This book belongs to:

_____

Published by Ladybird Books Ltd
A Penguin Company
Penguin Books Ltd, 80 Strand, London WC2R 0RL, UK
Penguin Books Australia Ltd, Camberwell, Victoria, Australia
Penguin Books (NZ) Ltd, Cnr Airbourne and Rosedale Roads, Albany, Auckland, 1310, New Zealand

1 3 5 7 9 10 8 6 4 2

© LADYBIRD BOOKS MMIV

Printed in Italy

Night
Animals

written by Lorraine Horsley
illustrated by Sharon Harmer

Ladybird

Night Animals

cat

owl

hyena

rabbit

frog

snake

turtle

platypus

bat

It is day.
The sun is in the sky
and children are playing
in the garden.

9

It is night.
The children are asleep
in bed. But in the dark,
a cat is awake.

whiskers to feel
in the dark

What other animals can you see?

11

It is night on the farm.
But in the dark, an owl
is flying over the fields.

big eyes to see
in the dark

What other animals can you see?

13

It is night on the grasslands
of Africa. But in the dark,
a hyena is looking
for food.

big nose to smell
in the dark

What other animals can you see?

It is night in the woods.
But in the dark, a rabbit
is listening for danger.

big ears to listen
in the dark

What other animals can you see?

It is night in the rainforest.
But in the dark, a frog
is calling for a mate.

big throat to call
and be heard in
the dark

What other animals can you see?

It is night in the desert.
But in the dark, a snake
is hiding.

heat sensor to feel
heat from animals
in the dark

What other animals can you see?

It is night on the beach.
But in the dark, a turtle
is laying her eggs.

laying eggs to be safe
from other animals
in the dark

It is night in the river.
But in the dark, a platypus
is swimming and looking
for food.

big bill to find
food in the dark

What other animals can you see?

It is night in the cave.
But in the dark, a baby
bat is learning to fly.

big ears to hear
sounds in the dark

Did you spot these night animals?

In the woods.

In the desert.

On the grasslands.

In the rainforest.

Index